<u>1001</u>

WAYS
TO BE A
Best
Friend

1001
WAYS
TO BE A
Best
Friend

NANCY KRULIK

SCHOLASTIC INC.
New York Toronto London Auckland Sydney

ISBN 0-590-91288-7

12 11 10 9 8 7 6 5 4 3 2 1   8 9/9 0 1 2 3/0

Printed in the U.S.A.   40

First Scholastic printing, February 1998

For Danny, my very best friend

Hanging Out

1. Watch the same TV shows, so you can talk about them later.

2. Stay on the phone with your best friend while you watch TV. That way you can watch the show together!

3. Let your best friend pick the movie.

4. Never see a movie with another friend after you've already promised to see it with your best friend.

5. Buy matching outfits.

6. Don't try to convince your best friend to buy something she can't afford.

7. Let your best friend have the last sweater

that's on sale. You can buy the next bar-
gain.

8. Take goofy pictures together in a photo
machine.

9. Try on lipsticks together at the makeup
counter.

10. Buy the same perfume.

11. Go to your favorite store and pick outfits
for each other to try on.

12. Go to the bead store together and make
matching bracelets.

13. Trade friendship bracelets.

14. # Try on
sunglasses
together.

15. Spend hours trying on hats together.

16. Invite your best friend along for a day at
the beach.

17. Help her pick a cool suit for the beach.

18. Be honest (but kind) if your best friend's bathing suit doesn't make her look her best.

19. Share the biggest beach umbrella in the world.

20. Put sunscreen on your best friend's back.

21. Ride the waves together.

22. Collect shells and make matching ankle bracelets.

23. Warn your best friend when she's getting too red from the sun.

24. Build a giant sand castle together.

25. Write your names in the sand.

26. Bury each other in the sand.

27. Win prizes for each other on the boardwalk.

28. Ride in the same car on a giant roller coaster.

29. Don't laugh if your best friend is afraid on the giant roller coaster.

30. Go sledding together.

31. Help your best friend pull the sled back up the hill.

32. Make snow angels together.

33. Work together to build the biggest snow-man in the neighborhood.

34. Start a snow-shoveling business together.

35. Start a lemonade stand together.

36. Always return anything you borrow.

37. Replace anything you borrow and destroy.

38. Make matching friendship pins.

39. Buy matching shoelaces for your sneakers.

40. Root for the same basketball team.

41. Laugh together over your best jokes.

42. Groan together over your worst jokes.

43. Don't tell jokes at your best friend's expense.

44. Go tubing down a river together.

45. Let your best friend sing out loud with the radio.

46. Request her favorite song on your local radio station.

47. Blow air kisses to each other, then try to catch them.

48. Watch your best friend's hamster while she's on vacation.

49. Sketch your best friend's portrait.

50. Help your best friend do her chores.

51. Keep your best friend's picture in your wallet.

52. Give her a picture of you for her wallet.

53. Go to a museum together.

54. Try to draw the pictures you see there.

55. Have lots of sleepovers.

56. Leave the light on for her during a sleep-over.

57. Never tell anyone your best friend is afraid of the dark.

58. Rent your favorite movies and have an all-night movie marathon.

59. Watch scary movies together.

60. Let your best friend know when the scary parts are over so she can look.

61. Have pillow fights.

62. Give your best friend the top bunk when she sleeps over.

63. Wash and style (but never cut!) your best friend's hair.

64. French-braid each other's hair.

65. Do each other's makeup.

66. Share fan magazines.

67. Take magazine quizzes together.

68. Write fan letters together.

69. Write a song together.

70. Write a book together.

71. Make up a new dance together.

72. Plant seeds and grow a garden together.

73. Help your best friend rearrange the furniture in her room.

74. Let your best friend have first pick of the babies in your gerbil's next litter.

75. Tape your best friend's favorite songs from your CDs.

76. Climb trees together.

77. Start a club.

78. Take turns being president and vice president.

79. Build a clubhouse.

80. Design a club flag.

81. Find out your best friend's horoscope sign.

82. See how much she is like her horoscope sign.

83. Start reading a book series together.

84. Grow a special "friendship plant" and give it to your best friend.

85. Go to the hairdresser with your best friend for moral support.

86. Go to the zoo together and make faces at the animals.

87. Go to the aquarium together and practice making fish faces.

88. Buy two tickets to the circus, and spend the day waving to the clowns.

89. Take music lessons together.

90. Start an all-girl band.

91. Don't call your best friend too late at night.

92. Don't call your best friend too early on weekend mornings.

93. Call each other on the phone — a lot.

94. Help your best friend baby-sit her little sister.

95. Introduce your best friend to your big brother's gorgeous best friend.

96. Volunteer as a team to read to the blind.

97. Volunteer together to work at a nursing home.

98. Volunteer together to help clean up a neighborhood park.

99. Compliment your best friend when she's not feeling too great about herself.

100. Practice saying tongue twisters until you are both laughing hysterically.

101. Trade CDs of your favorite music.

102. Trade CD-ROMs of your favorite computer games.

103. Share your favorite sweaters.

104. Trade earrings. (Sterilize them in alcohol before you put them on.)

105. With ticket stubs, photos, napkins, and more, make a collage of special days you've spent together.

106. Work together to put on a silly show for the neighborhood kids.

107. Take a knitting class together.

108. Knit scarves to keep each other warm.

109. Take a crochet class together.

110. Crochet hats for each other.

111. Say please when you ask for something.

112. Say thank you whenever you can.

113. Pick one day each week to be a special day with your best friend.

114. Play board games together.

115. Don't compete with each other.

116. Give your best friend the space to be herself.

117. Don't tempt your best friend to stay out later than she's allowed to.

118. Pick wildflowers together.

119. Dry the wildflowers in your memory books.

120. Dry rose petals and make potpourri bags for each other.

121. String flowers together to make Hawaiian leis for each other.

122. Be generous with your compliments.

123. Go together to meet the new kid on the block.

124. If you've been in your best friend's room all afternoon, help clean up before you go home.

125. Remind your best friend to buckle up during car trips.

126. Surprise your best friend by showing up at her dance recital.

127. Introduce your best friend to your favorite new band.

128. Listen to music by her favorite new band.

129. Camp out to-  gether — in your backyard.

130. Tell each other scary stories.

131. Start your own popular clique.

132. Make funny faces in the mirror together.

133. Write an episode of your favorite TV show together.

134. Put your best friend's phone number on your speed dial.

135. Don't brag.

136. Look on a map and imagine where you might both want to live someday.

137. Go to the library and read about those places.

138. Wear matching fake tattoos.

139. Get matching backpacks.

140. Memorize your best friend's E-mail address.

141. Send your best friend lots of E-mail.

142. Buy a book of brainteasers and solve them together.

143. Practice the newest dance moves together when no one is looking.

144. Never go on an afternoon talk show together.

145. Don't change the radio station when she's listening to her favorite song.

146. Take turns with the remote.

147. Build the world's tallest block tower.

148. If your best friend's folks say it's okay, help her paint her room.

149. Pretend you are both snakes wriggling on the ground or lions stalking a zebra in the tall grass.

150. Tie strings on your hands and feet. Be the marionette while your best friend is the puppeteer.

151. Now switch. You be the puppeteer while she's the marionette.

152. When you take pictures of a special day together, always make two copies.

153. Spend an afternoon together just looking at the clouds.

154. When you are alone, try to picture your best friend's room. Write down everything you remember.

155. If you see something that would look great in your best friend's room, buy it and surprise her.

156. Volunteer to help your best friend baby-sit.

157. If you can't take a baby-sitting job, recommend your best friend.

158. Never return anything you've borrowed in bad condition.

159. Don't do everything together. Give each other space.

160. Share your colored pencils. Then work together to make a rainbow.

161. Give your best friend a glass prism. Rainbows will follow her wherever she goes.

162. Pretend you're twins for a day.

163. Read the same mystery book.

164. Work together to solve the crime before you reach the last chapter.

165. Make a video about best friends.

166. Buy a book about handwriting analysis. See what your best friend's writing says about her.

167. Let your best friend see what your writing says about you, too.

168. # Rake leaves together.

169. Jump in the leaves together.

170. Make a picture using both of your fingerprints.

171. Learn to say each other's names . . . backward!

172. Find out where your families are originally from.

173. Learn about each other's heritage.

174. Work together to sculpt a clay monument to friendship.

175. Call before you drop by — even best friends need privacy.

176. Talk about your dream houses.

177. Learn to play chess together.

178. Buy a giant jigsaw puzzle and spend a whole month putting it together.

179. Create a new board game you can play together.

180. Make your best friend a Native American dream catcher to scare away her nightmares.

181. Work together to create your own comic strip about two best friends.

182. Help your best friend clean the junk out of her room.

183. Make a junk sculpture together.

184. Watch a sunset together.

185. Lie on the grass and look at the stars together.

186. Share a hammock on a hot day.

187. Run through the sprinkler together.

188. Catch frogs at the pond together.

189. Have a frog race. (Then put the frogs back in the pond.)

190. Walk barefoot in the grass together.

191. Jump in puddles together.

192. Make grass blade whistles and play a song together.

193. Dare to pretend.

194. Use a video camera to make commercials together.

195. Don't laugh when your best friend talks to characters on the TV screen.

196. Take turns pushing each other on the swings.

197. Make a train down a big slide together.

198. Have a conversation with your best friend while you are both hanging upside down on the jungle gym.

199. Sing "Row, Row, Row Your Boat" as a round.

200. Practice face painting on each other.

Chow Time!

201. Drink one milk shake with two straws.

202. Have a picnic in the park with your best friend.

203. Share your dessert at lunchtime.

204. Bake brownies together.

205. Go on a healthy diet together.

206. Invite your best friend to eat over when your mom is making your friend's favorite meal.

207. Invite her to eat over when her mom is making your friend's least favorite meal.

208. Give your best friend the last slice of pepperoni pizza.

209. Don't order ice cream if your best friend is on a diet.

210. Pack an extra sandwich, just in case her mom gives her liverwurst.

211. Always save a spot for your best friend at your lunch table.

212. Work together to make the biggest sandwich in the world. Then share it.

213. Loan your best friend lunch money if she's forgotten hers.

214. Pay back the lunch money she loaned you yesterday.

215. Share your last stick of gum.

216. Let your best friend pick the toppings for the pizza.

217. Share hot cocoa on freezing cold days.

218. Sip lemonade together on hot days.

219. When you're at the movies, buy the extra-large popcorn and share it.

220. Share your school lunch.

221. Collect and trade your favorite recipes.

222. Cook a shared meal, using all of your favorite recipes.

223. Grow gardens at each other's houses.

224. Make and share a big salad with vegetables from your gardens.

225. Make big ice cream sundaes for each other.

226. Bring your best friend a minibox of cereal for a before-school snack.

227. Have a traveling food party where you

stop at friends' houses for different courses.

228. Try food from foreign countries together.

229. Work together to learn to use chopsticks.

230. Bake cookies together for your school bake sale.

231. Bake cookies together and deliver them to a local homeless shelter.

232. Share the last brownie on the plate.

233. Make two big stacks of pancakes together and cover them in syrup.

234. Put together a best friends cookbook.

235. Let your best friend have the pink icing rose on the cake.

236. Split a double Popsicle from the ice cream truck.

237. Play tic-tac-toe on paper place mats in a restaurant.

238. Pick one song each on the restaurant juke-box.

239. Develop a secret passion for baby food ba-nanas. Promise not to tell!

240. Clank your water glasses together and say "Cheers!"

241. Share a bag of jelly beans and leave the red ones for last.

242. Have a pie-eating contest.

243. Pick strawberries together.

244. Share a bowl of fresh-picked strawberries and cream.

245. Bite off the bottom of your cones and see who can suck out the ice cream fastest.

246. Try to make the world's longest gum-wrapper chain.

247. Buy yourselves matching Pez candy dis-pensers.

248. Make two Froot Loops necklaces, one for you and one for her.

249. Snack on them all day.

250. Have an old-fashioned taffy pull.

251. Make super-chocolaty fudge together.

252. Take turns eating saltine crackers and trying to whistle.

253. After a bad day, share a container of ice cream using two spoons.

254. Give each other blindfolded taste tests to guess the flavors of Life Savers candies.

255. Divide animal cookies into pairs of the same animals.

256. Pull on the wishbone after Thanksgiving dinner.

257. Share a big box of chocolates.

258. Try to guess what's inside each chocolate before you each take a bite.

259. Split a bag of M&M's.

260. Try to eat all of the red ones first.

261. Share lots of different dishes at a Chinese restaurant.

262. Suck on candy canes and see who can make the sharpest point.

263. See who can reach the middle of the Tootsie Roll lollipop first. (Without biting!)

264. Let your best friend have the last, cheesiest, cheese fry.

265. Have six inches each of a Fruit-by-the-Foot candy.

266. Volunteer to taste your best friend's latest cooking experiment.

267. Dip slices of fruit in chocolate fondue together.

268. Smile at each other with orange section grins. (Put the section in your mouth so it covers your teeth.)

269. Make English muffin pizzas together.

270. Eat ice cream sundaes with your hands behind your backs.

271. Cut sandwiches into silly shapes and give them to each other.

272. Give your best friend your last breath mint because she's sitting next to a really cute guy.

273. You eat half of your blue cotton candy. Your best friend eats half of her pink one. Then you switch.

274. Order Shirley Temples in a restaurant.

275. Bake gingerbread girls that look like the two of you.

276. Eat outside and pretend you're lunching in a Paris cafe together.

277. Feed each other frozen grapes.

278. Have a spaghetti slurping contest.

279. Write each other's names with Alpha Bits cereal.

280. Find each other's initials in bowls of alphabet soup.

281. Decorate brown paper lunch bags for each other.

282. Bring your lunch to school in the bag your best friend made for you.

283. Twist marshmallows until you've both made ooey, gooey taffy.

284. Work together to arrange a box of Froot Loops by color before you eat them.

285. Give your best friend half of your chocolate pudding, take half of her vanilla pudding, and you'll each have a swirl for dessert.

286. Mix both of your favorite Kool-Aid flavors together in one pitcher.

Keeping Secrets

287. Make up a secret handshake.

288. Make up a secret language.

289. Write notes in code to your best friend.

290. Share secrets with each other.

291. Never tell your best friend's secrets.

292. Be there for your best friend when she needs a shoulder to cry on.

293. Be ready with a joke when she needs a good laugh.

294. Never tell a guy that your best friend likes him — unless she wants you to.

295. Defend your best friend if someone makes fun of her.

296. Give your best friend a diary as a gift.

297. Never read your best friend's diary.

298. Never go after your best friend's guy.

299. Best friends should never date the same people.

300. Choose your best friend over a boyfriend every time.

301. Don't lie to your best friend.

302. Don't tease your best friend.

303. When you play Truth or Dare, don't make the truth too painful or the dares too hard.

304. Go on quiet strolls through the woods so you can talk to each other in private.

305. Never judge your best friend.

306. Never talk about your best friend behind her back.

307. If your best friend doesn't want to talk about something, don't talk about it.

308. A good hug can stop a lot of tears.

309. Give each other secret names.

310. Give the kids at school secret names they'll never know about.

311. Let your feelings be known. Fight. But never fight in public.

312. Don't say things you don't mean.

313. Tell each other your dreams.

314. Never laugh at each other's dreams.

315. Keep private jokes.

316. Don't make promises you know you can't keep. *yes*

317. Don't do favors for credit. Help your best friend out because you want to. *yes*

318. Do something nice for your best friend, anonymously. *yes*

319. Be prepared to say "I'm sorry." *good*

320. Always be ready to forgive. *good*

321. Wish your best friend the same happiness you would wish for yourself. *yes*

322. Never get in the middle of a fight between your best friend and her parents. *bad to Fp*

323. Don't just hear your best friend's words. Listen to what she's really saying. *good*

324. Don't speak badly about others to your best friend. She may wonder what you're saying about her. *bad*

325. Write notes in invisible ink. *no*

326. Talk about your views of a perfect world.

327. Work together to make the world more perfect. *yes*

328. Dare each other to do something you've both always wanted to do. *yes*

329. Find out your best friend's favorite movie.

330. Rent the movie and watch it together.

331. Find out the name of your best friend's favorite actor.

332. Scan the TV listings, and give her a call when he's on the tube.

333. Secretly enter her in a contest to win a date with her favorite movie star.

334. Find out your best friend's favorite musical star.

335. Buy her that star's new CD for no reason at all.

336. Find out your best friend's favorite author.

337. Read a book by that author.

338. Find out your best friend's favorite food.

339. Find out what your best friend wants to be when she grows up.

340. Cut out any articles you see on her chosen profession, and give them to her.

341. Find out what your best friend is most afraid of.

342. Help her overcome her fears.

343. Find out what your best friend's goals are.

344. Help her achieve her goals.

345. Find out the one thing about your best friend that she is most proud of.

346. Be sure to compliment her (often) on her answer to the above.

347. Find out what your best friend would change about herself if she could.

348. Help her change it.

349. Find out what childhood toy your best friend wishes she could have again.

350. Buy it for her.

351. Share a laugh over the worst thing you've ever done together.

352. Recall the best thing you've ever done together.

353. Make a vow to do that thing again.

354. Tell your best friend how you like her hair best.

355. Admit to being jealous over something your friend has.

356. Now get over it.

357. Trust each other.

358. Respect your best friend's decisions.

359. Make wishes for each other on dandelion fluffs.

360. Don't tell anyone that your best friend is afraid of thunder.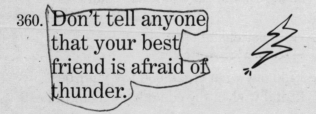

361. Learn to say "Never mind."

362. Say "No problem" as often as possible.

363. Develop a taste for humble pie.

364. Pretend you've found Aladdin's lamp. Ask each other what you'd wish for.

365. Pinky swear.

366. Vow to be roommates when you grow up and go away to college.

367. Don't offer advice until it's asked for.

368. Share a secret place with her.

369. Learn sign language so you can tell secrets without anyone hearing.

370. Don't tell anyone you both cry at sad movies sometimes.

371. *Really* don't tell anyone you both cry at *Brady Bunch* reruns sometimes.

372. Have a secret telephone code.

373. Admit that you still believe in unicorns, sort of.

374. Start a "penny for your thoughts" jar together.

375. When you have enough pennies, go out and
do something really special together.

376. Make up a secret knock.

377. Reveal your most embarrassing moments
to each other.

378. Don't laugh when your best friend reveals
her most embarrassing moment.

379. Make up a secret word.

380. Write the secret word all over your
notebooks.

381. Let others try to figure out what your secret word means.

382. Say "Cross my heart and hope to die"
whenever you make promises to each
other.

Go Team!

383. Go hiking together.

384. Root for the same baseball team on TV.

385. Have a Super Bowl party.

386. Be there to cheer for your best friend when she tries out for a team.

387. Take up tennis together.

388. Be tennis doubles partners.

389. Play a little one-on-one basketball.

390. Play catch together outside.

391. Go jogging with your best friend.

392. Go on long bike rides together.

393. Remind your best friend to wear a helmet when she rides.

394. Practice cartwheels together.

395. Help your best friend learn a good racing dive.

396. Collect and trade baseball cards with each other.

397. Go with your best friend to cheer on her brother's Little League team.

398. Spend an evening playing miniature golf together.

399. Join a gym together.

400. Do workout tapes together.

401. Be in the stands when your best friend plays a school sport.

402. Go out for the same sport.

403. Don't be jealous if your best friend makes the team and you don't.

404. Volunteer together to work at the Special Olympics.

405. Sign up together for a charity walk-athon.

406. Sign up together for a charity bike-athon.

407. Sign up together for a charity skate-athon.

408. Go ice-skating together.

409. Go Rollerblading together.

410. Remind your best friend to wear her helmet and wrist and knee guards.

411. Go on power walks together.

412. Take self-defense classes together.

413. Have a snowball fight.

414. Buy matching sweatbands.

415. Tape the big game for your best friend if she can't watch it.

416. Take turns holding each other's feet while you both practice handstands.

417. Spot each other.

418. Play catch with a water balloon.

419. Take your best friend's picture as she crosses the finish line.

420. Give her a blue ribbon — even if she doesn't win the race.

421. Fly kites together in an open field.

422. Enter a three-legged race together.

423. Spend a rainy afternoon together at the bowling alley.

424. Don't laugh at your best friend's gutter balls.

425. Cheer her strikes and spares.

426. Spend a stormy afternoon playing waste-paper basketball together in your room.

427. Have a jacks marathon.

428. Field each other's grounders.

429. Always play fair.

430. If you win and your best friend doesn't, remember to give her a big "Two, four, six, eight, who do we appreciate?"

431. Don't be a sore loser.

432. Be buddies for free swim.

433. Go fishing together, and don't care if you don't catch anything.

434. Sometimes let her tag you when she's "it."

435. Work as a team to try to break a world's record.

436. Learn to twirl batons.

437. Be there when your best friend makes her first jump off the high-dive.

438. Put matching cards in your bicycle tires so you can both *click, click, click* as you ride.

439. Let your best friend play the last ball in the pinball game.

440. Make up a new cheer together.

441. Sign each other's sneakers.

442. Share a ride on a ski lift.

443. Row a boat by each taking one oar.

444. Make up a two-person juggling routine.

445. Play badminton together.

446. Play volleyball together on the sand at the beach.

447. Make up a synchronized swimming routine.

448. Play Follow the Leader. Take turns being the leader.

449. Be each other's partner for square dancing in gym class.

450. Teach each other the right words to "The Star-Spangled Banner."

451. Sing it really loudly the next time you go to a ball game together.

452. Play Kick the Can together.

453. Have a Ping-Pong tournament.

454. Rent a bicycle built for two.

455. Run a race together for moral support.

456. Jump together with one rope.

457. Fly kites together.

458. Play handball together on your garage door.

459. Have a doggie-paddle race.

460. Play Freeze Tag in the sprinkler.

Keep in Touch

461. Send your best friend a letter *before* she leaves for camp.

462. Mail the daily horoscope to her at camp.

463. While she's away at camp without TV, send her the weekly soap opera updates.

464. Keep a journal of things you want to tell your best friend when she returns.

465. Mail her postcards from places you visit on vacation.

466. Send her pictures of you while you're on vacation.

467. Tape your best friend's favorite TV shows so she can watch them when she gets back.

468. Start a neighborhood newsletter and mail it to her.

469. Send each other videos of yourselves.

470. Call each other once a week if you can.

471. Trade long-distance call costs. You call one week, she calls the next.

472. Fax each other silly pictures.

473. Play chess through the mail.

474. Mail each other hair ribbons to wear.

475. Send her a care package filled with her favorite treats and a picture of you.

476. Mail her a care package filled with mini-soaps and shampoos.

477. Write each other letters on matching stationery.

478. Mail your best friend stickers.

479. Send her a package of wacky comic books.

480. Promise to stop what you're doing and think of each other at six-fifteen every night.

481. Make beaded necklaces for each other. Add one bead for every night you're apart.

482. Buy matching lockets to wear when you are apart.

483. Send your best friend a letter glued to cardboard and cut apart like a jigsaw puzzle.

484. Write a continuing story and mail it back and forth all summer.

485. Sign some letters: UR2Good2B4Gotten.

486. Sign some letters: Best Friends 4-Ever.

487. Try to visit your best friend at camp on visiting day.

488. Give her your teddy bear to sleep with while she is away.

489. Bring her key chains from the places you've visited.

490. Bring her refrigerator magnets from the places you've visited.

491. If you're lonely, close your eyes and picture your best friend smiling at you.

492. Keep this old saying in mind: Absence makes the heart grow fonder.

493. Wear half-of-a-heart necklaces.

494. Make a tape of the two of you singing so she can play it wherever she goes.

495. Remember to say "I missed you" when you meet up again.

496. Make your best friend something special in arts and crafts.

497. Spend a week at your best friend's new house.

498. Send her a video tour of your new house.

499. Give her a gift to open when she's on the plane.

School Days

500. Be nervous together on the first day of school.

501. Save your best friend a seat on the bus.

502. Always sit in the two seats at the back of the bus.

503. Let her have the window seat.

504. Write your names backward on the steamed-up bus windows.

505. Walk to school together.

506. Walk home together.

507. Sit together in class.

508. Help your best friend with her English homework.

509. Let her help you with your math homework.

510. Sign up to do group projects together.

511. Study for tests together.

512. Go to the library together after school.

513. Read the same library books.

514. Make up an act together for the school talent show.

515. Help your best friend learn her lines for the school play.

516. Bake your best friend a batch of cookies to munch on while she's cramming for a big test.

517. Buy her a big map to help her with geography.

518. Volunteer to be her lab partner, even if she's awful in science.

519. Join the school chorus together.

520. Try to get on the same teams in gym class.

521. If your best friend wants the job, nominate her for an office in student government.

522. Be her campaign manager.

523. Bring an extra pencil just in case your best friend forgets hers.

524. Compare and share notes before the big test.

525. Make your best friend funky bookplates for her schoolbooks.

526. Let your best friend cut in front of you in the lunch line.

527. Offer your best friend your favorite book for her book report.

528. Learn to jump double Dutch together at recess.

529. Make a lamp in shop class for your best friend's room.

530. Be the first ones to sign each other's autograph books.

531. Loan your best friend your lucky shirt to wear on the day of her big spelling test.

532. Wear one blue sock and one red sock each to school.

533. Pass each other notes in the hall (but not during class!).

534. Help fix the glitch in your best friend's computer program.

535. Stay on the phone together until you hear if it's a snow day.

536. Learn a foreign language together.

537. Speak in that language when you don't want anyone to know what you're saying.

Celebrations

538. Never forget your best friend's birthday.

539. Buy her a birthday present you would like to get.

540. Bake her a birthday cake.

541. Help her blow out the candles.

542. Throw your best friend a surprise party.

543. Be the loudest one when everyone sings "Happy Birthday."

544. Be a singing telegram with a song you wrote just for her birthday.

545. Be the first to come and the last to leave at your best friend's birthday party.

546. Make your best friend an "It's My Birthday" corsage to wear at her party.

547. Take your time picking out the perfect birthday card.

548. If you can't find the perfect card, make it yourself.

549. Remember to mail your card so it gets there on time.

550. Write a special poem for your best friend's birthday.

551. Give your best friend gifts with a theme (like ballet, music, or art).

552. Cover her gift with lots and lots of ribbons and bows.

553. Don't take a picture of your best friend in the goofy birthday hat her mother made her wear.

554. Don't give her birthday smacks.

555. Don't encourage other people to give her birthday smacks.

556. Don't wait till the last minute to think of a gift. Keep a list of ideas all year long.

557. Paint a gold star on a T-shirt and give it to your best friend as a gift. She's a real star!

558. Wrap her present in pictures of her favorite movie star.

559. Instead of one big gift, give her a few little ones — all wrapped separately.

560. If you can't afford a gift, give her an IOU for help with homework or chores.

561. Put a limit on how much you will spend on each other's holiday gift.

562. Go caroling together and try to sing in harmony.

563. Make your best friend an extra-large Christmas stocking with her name on it.

564. Trim your best friend's tree with her.

565. Make sure your best friend and the guy she likes wind up under the mistletoe at the same time.

566. String popcorn to make Christmas decorations together.

567. Volunteer together to give out holiday gifts at a local family shelter.

568. Give each other best friend Christmas ornaments.

569. Buy each other matching charms for your charm bracelets.

570. Give your best friend hand-dipped Hanukkah candles.

571. Have a super sleepover to ring in the New Year.

572. Call your best friend at midnight to wish her a happy New Year.

573. Never return a gift from your best friend.

574. Give your best friend a carnation on Valentine's Day.

575. Make Valentine's Day cards out of construction paper and lace.

576. Go on an Easter egg hunt together.

577. Spend a day together painting Easter eggs.

578. Split a chocolate Easter bunny.

579. Don't play April Fool's Day tricks on each other.

580. On May 1, surprise each other with May baskets full of spring flowers.

581. Go to the neighborhood Fourth of July fireworks together.

582. On Halloween, dress as a pair (Laurel and Hardy, Batman and Robin . . .).

583. On Halloween, slip into one big shirt and go as a two-headed monster.

584. Make matching Halloween masks.

585. Share your Halloween candy.

586. Plan a big Halloween party together.

587. Make handmade pumpkin invitations together.

588. Make sure your best friend carries a flashlight for safety when you trick-or-treat at night.

589. Go pumpkin-picking together.

590. Carve your pumpkins into really scary jack-o'-lanterns.

591. Make grave rubbings together on Halloween night.

592. On Thanksgiving Day, be sure to tell your pal you're thankful she's your best friend.

593. Dress up as a Pilgrim for her Thanksgiving video project.

594. Don't leave your best friend to be a wallflower at the school dance.

595. If you go to the dance with your best friend, be sure you leave with her, too.

596. Don't go to a party if your best friend isn't invited, too.

597. Celebrate National Nothing Day (January 16). Spend it vegging out together.

598. Remember, cash is generally not a good gift for a best friend.

599. Give each other valentines . . . in July!

600. Convince each other that Friday the thirteenth is a *good* luck day.

601. See how long you both can keep a balloon in the air.

602. Have an un-birthday party together.

To Your Health

603. Bring your best friend a big pot of chicken soup when she's ill.

604. If your best friend is sick in bed, call her every once in a while just to show you care.

605. Rent some silly videos your best friend can watch while she recuperates.

606. Bring her flowers.

607. Send her silly get well cards.

608. Bring over a big stack of magazines.

609. Bring over a book on tape.

610. Be the first one to sign your best friend's cast.

611. **Carry her books while she's on crutches.**

612. Volunteer to help wash her hair if she isn't able to shower.

613. Hand-deliver a glass of fresh-squeezed orange juice.

614. Remember to fill her in on all the school gossip she's missed.

615. Bring a new lipstick, so your best friend can look great even though she's sick.

616. Stay healthy. Your best friend needs you.

617. Fill a notebook with some of the funniest

jokes you know. Laughter is the best
medicine.

618. Think of simple word games, like Twenty
Questions, which you can play on the
phone.

619. Help your sick best friend fill in the pages
of her movie star scrapbook.

620. Go to the dentist with your best friend for
moral support.

621. Always remember to say "Bless you!"
when your best friend sneezes.

622. Go out and celebrate a doctor's appoint-
ment with no shots!

623. Bring your best friend ice cream after she's
had her tonsils out.

624. Assure your best friend that her appendix
scar is really neat!

625. Volunteer together to be candy stripers at
the local hospital.

626. Feed your fish.

627. Clean out your hamster's cage.

628. Make sure your pet's cage is large enough to keep it happy.

629. Let your bird fly once in a while.

630. Don't walk your dog over any rock salt.

631. Pet your puppy for no reason at all.

632. Take your dog for long walks in quiet woods.

633. Give your dog frequent baths.

634. Keep your cat away from houseplants.

635. Let your cat sleep on your pillow some-times.

636. Surprise your cat with a toy from the pet shop.

637. Give your cat a big ball of yarn to play with.

638. Don't leave your pets alone for too long a time.

639. Take your pet to the vet for its checkup.

640. Put out a bird feeder in your backyard.

641. Make sure your dogs and cats wear collars.

642. Be grateful for those wet, sloppy dog kisses.

643. Choose a name your pet can be proud of.

644. Slip your dog his favorite scraps under the table.

645. Play Frisbee with your pooch.

646. Use your allowance money to adopt an animal at the local zoo.

647. Tell your pets they're loved.

648. Take up bird-watching as a hobby.

649. Volunteer at the local ASPCA.

650. Let the dog up on the couch once in a while.

651. Take your dog to a local dog run where it can make some puppy pals.

652. Give your guinea pig fresh water every day.

653. Sing back to your canary.

654. Stencil the words *Good Dog* on your puppy's water bowl.

655. Plump up the pillows in your puppy's doggie bed.

Brotherly (and Sisterly) Love!

656. Kiss your little brother or sister often.

657. Hugs are free, but they mean a lot to a younger sibling.

658. Keep your side of the room neat.

659. Read your little brother a bedtime story when you can.

660. Take your little sister to the playground.

661. Don't use your little brother or sister as a gofer.

662. Remember, little kids are people, too.

663. Don't tease your little sister about her first crush.

664. Every once in a while, surprise your small sib with a small gift — maybe a pack of baseball cards or a candy necklace.

665. If your older brother is studying for finals, help out by doing his chores.

666. Help your older brother wash his car.

667. Get a family exercise class going.

668. Don't take over the bathroom.

669. If your big sister has a date over, say hi. Then leave.

670. Don't take anything from anybody's room without asking.

671. Respect your sibling's privacy.

672. Knock on the door before you come in.

673. Take the time to ask your sister how her day went.

674. Don't treat your big brother's wallet like a bank.

675. Give your big sister a surprise phone call at college.

676. Share the greatest gift of all — your time.

677. Don't be the one to spill the beans about the Tooth Fairy and Santa Claus.

678. Be the patient when your little sister wants to use her doctor kit.

679. Let your big brother have the "corner part" of the couch sometimes.

680. Don't listen in on your big sister's phone conversations.

681. Patch the knees on your little brother's jeans.

682. Put a hook where your little sister can reach it, so she can hang up her own coat.

683. Write down your little sister's wish list for Santa.

684. Really mail her list to Santa, care of the North Pole.

685. Take your little brother to visit a fire station.

686. Help your little sister learn to ride a bike without training wheels.

687. Wash your little brother's security blanket, and have it back on his bed before he notices it's missing.

688. Try not to tie up the family phone.

689. Give your little brother a copy of a book you loved when you were his age.

690. Let your little sister crawl in your bed after she's had a bad dream.

691. Let your little brother hold your hamster.

692. Sew a dress for your sister's Barbie doll.

693. Spend a rainy afternoon helping your little brother make a parking lot with all his cars.

694. Treat your little sister to her first pony ride.

695. Keep your opinions on your big sister's friends to yourself.

Parents as Pals

696. Run errands.

697. Offer to help without having to be asked.

698. Clean up your room.

699. Surprise your folks with breakfast in bed.

700. After a late snack, rinse off the dishes and put them away.

701. Say "I love you" for no reason at all except that you do.

702. Copy Mom's recipes on index cards and store them in a box.

703. Don't run to Dad for permission when Mom has already said no.

704. Don't cut up Dad's favorite magazine before he's had the chance to read it.

705. At the library, pick up a book you think your dad might like.

706. Crochet a few "mittens" for your parents' golf clubs.

707. Pick out mother/daughter outfits you and Mom can wear together.

708. Give your parents five minutes to collect their thoughts when they walk in the door after work.

709. Bring your dad a cool glass of lemonade while he's cooking burgers on a hot grill.

710. Don't laugh at your parents' old-fashioned music.

711. Spend an afternoon putting family pictures in an album.

712. Call if you're going to be late.

713. Don't complain about going to visit your great-aunt Ida.

714. Wipe off your dog's muddy paws before he walks on the nice clean floor.

715. Be home in time for family dinners.

716. Don't ask "Are we there yet?" on long car trips.

717. Watch an old black-and-white movie on TV with your dad.

718. **Go out for a fancy tea with your mom.**

719. Surprise your dad by shining his shoes.

720. Clip coupons from the Sunday paper and put them in a little envelope for your parents to take to the market.

721. Do the dishes so your mom can watch that movie she's been dying to see.

722. Bring your dad a cup of hot coffee when he's shoveling the snow.

723. Bring your mom a cool glass of iced tea when she's gardening in the hot sun.

724. Ask your mom to teach you some dances from when she was a kid.

725. Don't refer to the time when your mom was a kid as "the olden days."

726. Ask permission before you raid your dad's closet looking for a new nightshirt.

727. Convince your parents (or anyone you love) to stop smoking.

Make Every Day Grandparent's Day

728. Give your grandparents a surprise visit (or phone call) for no reason at all.

729. Volunteer to take your grandparents' dog for a long walk.

730. Make a quilt or crochet an afghan with your grandmother.

731. Remember Grandma on Mother's Day.

732. Remember Grandpa on Father's Day.

733. If your grandparents live far away, take some family photos, put them in an album, and mail them off. Grandparents love to see how you've grown.

734. Fax your grandparents a copy of your A+ book report.

735. Help Grandma cook her secret recipe.

736. Ask to hear stories about when your parents were young.

737. Ask to hear stories about when your grandparents were young.

738. Let your grandmother push your bangs off your forehead.

Be Your Own Best Friend

739. Cut yourself some slack. Nobody's perfect.

740. Pamper yourself with a long bath after a hard day.

741. Accept your body as it is.

742. Don't compare yourself to others.

743. If you give it your best shot, that's enough.

744. Don't be afraid to ask for help.

745. Eat right.

746. Exercise often.

747. Treat yourself to your favorite dessert once in a while.

748. Learn from your mistakes.

749. Rejoice in your successes.

750. Don't wallow in your failures.

751. Allow yourself time to cry.

752. Make sure you take the time to smile.

753. Use your head.

754. Follow your heart.

755. Buy yourself flowers.

756. Wear a jacket when it's cold.

757. Work hard.

758. Play hard.

759. Dream.

760. Open your heart to others.

761. Open your mind to new ideas.

762. Overcome shyness.

763. Keep your sense of humor.

764. Learn to say no when you need to.

765. Believe in yourself.

766. Develop your own style.

767. Take a hot bath
after a
long day.

768. Find a private place where you can sit
alone and think.

769. Convince yourself that the best is yet to
come.

770. Learn at least one new thing every day.

771. Remember that it's okay to talk to yourself
so long as no one is listening.

772. Go for it!

773. Remember that it's really never too late to
learn anything.

774. Keep thinking.

775. Draw a self-portrait.

776. Hold on to your dignity.

777. Set goals for yourself.

778. At the end of the day, think of one thing you did well.

779. Congratulate yourself.

780. Take one hour a day all for yourself.

Mother Earth Needs Best Friends

781. Recycle.

782. Take your bikes, not the car.

783. Plant trees.

784. Take a shower instead of a bath.

785. Pick up litter.

786. Make a compost pile.

787. Use recycled paper.

788. Wash clothes in warm water, not hot water.

789. Bring a reusable cloth bag to the grocery store.

790. Cut your old jeans into new shorts.

791. Volunteer to work with a group that tries to save endangered animals.

792. Use only returnable bottles.

793. Set the table with cloth napkins.

794. Put a fresh coat of paint on your old furniture.

795. Wrap gifts in the comic pages from the Sunday paper.

796. Use rechargeable batteries.

797. Join your school's ecology club.

798. If your school doesn't have an ecology club, start one.

799. Turn off the light when you leave the room.

800. Don't leave the water running while you brush your teeth.

801. With your best friend, look up unusual words in the dictionary.

802. Use your new words and show everyone how smart you both are.

803. Have a staring contest.

804. Have a quiet contest.

805. Don't be jealous if your best friend hangs out with other kids, too.

806. Let your best friend have the heads-up penny you spotted at the same time.

807. Enjoy the times you feel you're the only two people in the world.

808. Sing "One Hundred Bottles of Pop on the Wall," all the way through.

809. Spend a rainy day together playing hide-and-seek.

810. Take turns tossing coins into a fountain.

811. Sign your names with the same symbol (a heart, a peace sign, or a flower).

812. Let your best friend fall asleep on your shoulder on the way home.

813. Have Slinky races down the front stairs.

814. Spend the day together at the park, feeding the pigeons.

815. Keep a journal of your times together.

816. Put on white shirts and yell "Hey, you in the white shirt!" to each other.

817. Help your best friend start the box stitch on her lanyard.

818. Catch fireflies together.

819. Set them free together.

820. Put books on both your heads and practice walking with perfect posture.

821. Pool your allowance money and mail away for Sea Monkeys.

822. Lie down under a tree together and watch the leaves blow.

823. Spray each other with Silly String.

824. Sew matching patches on your jean jackets.

825. Let your best friend hear the ocean in your biggest shell.

826. Carry matching metal lunch boxes as pocketbooks.

827. Let a ladybug crawl from your best friend's finger to yours.

828. Try facial masks together.

829. Don't laugh at each other while you're wearing the facial masks.

830. Make rag dolls that look like each other.

831. On a hot day, spray each other with water from the hose.

832. Make comb-and-wax-paper kazoos.

833. Play your kazoos along with the radio.

834. Go through all of the stages of cat's cradle together.

835. Hang out on a hayride.

836. Bury each other in the hay.

837. Watch a parade together.

838. Lift each other up to see the parade floats better.

839. Let your best friend have heads when you toss a coin.

840. After a big storm, go outside together to search for a rainbow.

841. Work together to capture caterpillars and watch them turn into butterflies.

842. Sit quietly together and watch a butterfly walk across a leaf.

843. Share the last horse on the merry-go-round.

844. Put on ten-gallon hats and pretend to be cowgirls.

845. Use your lassos to rope a tree stump.

846. Watch the Academy Awards together.

847. Laugh together at the dresses the actresses wear to the Academy Awards.

848. Find out what each other's names mean.

849. Give your best friend a swatch of your old flannel shirt as a square for her new quilt.

850. Swap the clothes you're tired of wearing.

851. Switch seats every now and then at the movies, so that neither of you is stuck for the whole show behind the lady with the hat.

852. Press the OPEN button on the elevator so your best friend can make it before the doors shut.

853. Send your best friend a letter once in a while, just so she'll get some mail.

854. Get dressed up, even though you both have nowhere to go.

855. Find somewhere to go now that you're both dressed up.

856. Give each other manicures.

857. Give each other pedicures.

858. Promise each other you'll wear nothing but purple for a whole week.

859. Sit together for hours and watch a spider spin its web.

860. Loan your best friend an umbrella to go home with.

861. **Send off a message from the two of you in a bottle.**

862. Weave daisies into each other's hair.

863. Take each other's picture at the same date, time, and place every year.

864. Always be on time.

865. Don't let arguments go on for too long.

866. Make sure your best friend calls home when she's supposed to.

867. Take up stamp collecting as a hobby. Trade stamps.

868. Exchange baby pictures.

869. Help your best friend find the last word in her word search puzzle.

870. Spend hours together in the bookstore.

871. Help each other practice walking gracefully in high heels.

872. Count up the years, months, days, and hours you've been best friends. It will take you many, many minutes.

873. Go window-shopping when you're both really broke.

874. On a warm rainy day, go outside, shampoo your hair, and share a laugh.

875. Write to pen pals in another state who are best friends, too.

876. Make your best friend's number the very first one you dial when you get your own phone.

877. Pretend you are your best friend's reflection in the mirror.

878. Let her pretend to be your reflection in the mirror, too.

879. Look at your best friend through a kaleidoscope.

880. Let her look at you through a kaleidoscope.

881. Share a good luck charm. Hold on to it only when you need it.

882. Practice hand-clapping rhymes until you can go really, really fast.

883. Treat your best friend's parents with respect.

884. Go see your first live show together.

885. Have a food fight.

886. Clean up together after the food fight.

887. Teach your parakeet to say your best friend's name.

888. Glue your best friend's picture to the cover of her favorite star-studded magazine.

889. Help your best friend find her missing house keys.

890. Tape a long roll of paper to the wall and paint a mural together.

891. Synchronize your watches.

892. Stand back-to-back, link arms, and walk like an octopus.

893. Push each other around in a wheelbarrow.

894. Wait in line together to meet your favorite singing stars.

895. Watch a silent movie together. Make up funny things the actors could be saying.

896. Count the number of steps between your house and your best friend's.

897. Try to read each other's palms.

898. Get twenty-five-cent prizes from a gumball machine and trade them.

899. Pool your CDs and play radio station all afternoon.

900. Walk in each other's footsteps in the fresh snow.

901. Go to a free concert together in the park.

902. Spin each other around in a turning chair.

903. Let your best friend keep the prize in the Cracker Jack box.

904. Walk in the woods together and collect leaves for leaf prints.

905. Make two boats from newspaper together.

906. Float them in the lake.

907. Let your best friend have the last word once in a while.

908. Use pots and spoons to beat out the pattern of the rain on the roof together.

909. Skip over the cracks in the sidewalk arm in arm.

910. Make up silly lyrics to popular songs together.

911. Help each other pump air into your bicycle tires.

912. Watch *Sesame Street* together for old time's sake.

913. Play Twister.

914. Search your best friend's attic for ghosts.

915. Make lists of what you'll each name your future kids.

916. Try to make blueprints of each other's houses.

917. Play "Heart and Soul" together on the piano.

918. Wear matching toe rings with sandals.

919. Tie-dye shirts in matching colors.

920. Let your best friend dip her napkin in your glass of seltzer to get the stain off her white pants.

921. Have a Crazy Eights card marathon together.

922. Watch *The Wizard of Oz* together. Say the words at the same time the actors do.

923. Hang upside down from a low tree limb and pretend you're bats.

924. Try on mood lipstick to see if you are in the same mood.

925. Clap with one hand each.

926. Invite your best friend along for the first ride in your family's new car.

927. Hold the skein still while your best friend rolls a ball of yarn.

928. Trace each other's silhouette.

929. Cut out the words from a comic strip and write your own captions.

930. Spend the whole day speaking in pig Latin.

931. Blow straw wrappers at each other.

932. Slip ice down each other's backs in the summertime.

933. Catch snowflakes on your tongues.

934. Try to catch squirrels by climbing a tree and acting like nuts.

935. Wear blue shorts and a white shirt when your best friend wears white shorts and a blue shirt.

936. Search the rocks in your best friend's garden for fossil remains.

937. Play leapfrog together.

938. See who can blow the biggest bubble gum bubble.

939. Use peanut butter to get the bubble gum out of each other's hair.

940. Whirl around and around until you both get dizzy.

941. Roll down a hill together.

942. Go to the pet store together and make animal noises.

943. Give each other piggyback rides.

944. Pretend you're living a long time ago. Spend the day together using no electricity.

945. Play the word game G*H*O*S*T even when it's not Halloween.

946. Once in a while, be the "rotten egg" who is the last one in.

947. Let your best friend borrow your blue scarf, which would look great with her new shirt.

948. Make a best friends' time capsule. Fill it with notes and souvenirs of things you've done together.

949. Remember to open the time capsule when you are both thirty-five.

950. In a rainstorm, use one magazine to cover your heads.

951. Laugh at yourselves in an amusement park hall of mirrors.

952. If your best friend is too short to ride the loop-the-loop, wait until next year.

953. Dress up in sheet-togas and pretend you are both in ancient Rome.

954. See whose rock can make the most "skips" on the water.

955. Wear matching red suspenders to school.

956. Stand behind your best friend. Put your arms through hers. Move your hands while she talks.

957. Next time, you do the talking while she moves the hands.

958. Give her your favorite Snow White pillowcase when she sleeps over.

959. Get together to sing camp songs in January.

960. Listen to your best friend complain without complaining.

961. Come over when your best friend has to play with that really obnoxious kid who is her mother's best friend's son.

962. Turn up the radio really loud when your best friend's favorite song comes on.

963. Wear a button with a picture of the two of you on it.

964. Grow your bangs out together.

965. Let your best friend hold your four-leaf clover in her pocket during her math quiz.

966. Have a splash fight in the pool on a hot summer day.

967. Bury each other up to your necks in an indoor playground ball pit.

968. Go back and visit the place where you first met.

969. See what you both remember about the day you first met.

970. Step on each other's brand-new sneakers to scuff them up just right.

971. Take pictures of each other posing like famous statues.

972. Join hands and jump on sheets of bubble wrap.

973. Watch an old Marx Brothers movie, then try to act out the routines.

974. Play Name That Tune with your favorite songs.

975. Wrap your hair in towels like turbans, and pretend to be elegant ladies.

976. Pretend you both know how to tap dance.

977. Practice being rock stars and use hairbrushes for microphones.

978. Rub a comb on your sweater and make each other's hair stand on end.

979. Use Popsicle sticks to build memory boxes for each other.

980. Share a big blanket at a football game.

981. Fill a kiddie pool with bubbles and take a bubble bath together in your bathing suits.

982. Make like a silent movie. Blink the lights on and off quickly while your best friend dances.

983. Yell out "Jinx! You owe me a Coke!" when you say the same thing at the same time.

984. Throw up a fleet of maple-seed one-winged helicopters.

985. Put your hands over your best friend's eyes and say "Guess who!"

986. Take care of her virtual pet for the weekend and push all the right buttons.

987. Don't make fun of your best friend's middle name, which she hates.

988. Read the Sunday comics at the same time.

989. Wait until your best friend is finished reading to turn the page.

990. Take no for an answer.

991. Share your binoculars in the "nosebleed" section of the ballpark.

992. Get a rubber stamp made with both of your names on it.

993. Shampoo up each other's hair and make soap sculptures.

994. Loan your best friend a beautiful bow on a bad hair day.

995. Take turns being the stern in the canoe.

996. Walk away from the bad kids together.

997. Look through catalogs together.

998. Imagine what you'd buy from the catalogs if you both had the money.

999. Have your favorite photo of the two of you blown up into a poster for your best friend.

1000. Pop each other's soap bubbles.

1001. Give your best friend a copy of this book.